Go Home

poems

Hannu Afere

Ala Africa Books
Published by Ala Africa Ltd.
1st Floor, North Westgate House, Harlow, Essex,
United Kingdom. CM20 1YS

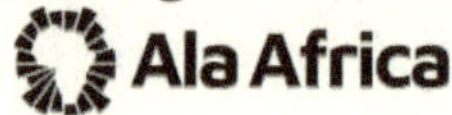

USA | UK | Nigeria

GO HOME

An Ala Africa Book / published by Ala Africa Ltd.

Book design by Dhee Sylvester.

ISBN: 979-8-9927448-2-8

for Ebimoboere.

love, confidante & fierce, fierce friend.

Author's Note

Imagine this: you're in 2077. All the tech billionaires have blown your dreams to heaven. And your native Gods intervene to stop you from getting caught in the crossfire, and they build you a sanctuary. So for all the times people abroad told you to go back to where you came from… you return.

And your Gods are not cruel capitalists or wicked dictators. If anything, they are hyper-aware of how history has framed them. Perhaps it is all because of respectability politics, or internalized coloniality, or the postcolonial anxiety of perception; they overcorrect. Your Gods open the gates wide. Refugees enter but so do opportunists. Soon the city goes from safe haven to möbius jungle where even the Òrìṣà hesitate. Alleys breathe with the stink of untreated sewage and emergent microbial pantheons, rats wearing crowns of aluminum foil post conspiracies on the net, humans barter with panic and illusion, some who bless you sharpen knives in their mouths, some who smile are ready taste your blood, all lizards crawl on stomachs but which is aching? And a sure-fire way of getting lynched is by saying out loud: "This city is no man's land."

People are still proud of their roots and history however spotted. Which begs the question: if a community defines itself strongly enough, does it automatically produce someone who does not fit? If so, then xenophobia may not be an accident at all, but a structural feature of identity. That is the terrifying implication. Rebellions begin in the underground, and innocent migrants + returnees are caught in the middle.

Ọṣùn's domains: the wellness clinics, aesthetic augmentation parlors, diplomatic embassies, are soon hijacked by the counter government. Ogun's foundries, the world-class roads stitching the metropolis together, the dock cranes moving freight with ritual precision, are a thing of beauty spoiled.

In the Egúngún Archive Sector, ancestral cloud servers are housed in sanctified temples. Here, families can commune with digitized lineage. Ghosts meant to find forever homes, are used for bad juju. The only sector still relatively uncorrupted is the powerstation Ṣàngó and his wives built, the hydroelectric facility boasts an installed capacity of 45,000 megawatts, utilizing 62 massive turbines.

All this for a people who just a few years ago in 2026, were still suffering from collapsing grids and epileptic power supply!

This is the world I built in my head to answer the questions: What legitimizes authority? Gods? Infrastructure? Nukes? What if technology and divinity are not opposites? Can one protect cultural identity without becoming exclusionary? Is global openness compatible with deep local belonging?

Can a people ever return to a pre-colonial identity, or is identity permanently altered by domination? Is home geography, memory, ancestry, or recognition? If you return and feel estranged, is it still home? How does trauma produce fear? How does fear become policy? If I have to listen to one more indigenes vs citizens vs state of origin debate, I might have to eat my ears! Perhaps home is the only place where you can become the thing you once feared—and must decide, daily, not to.

And that is the terror.

Hannu Afere

1.1.26

CONTENT

1. what even is home?
2. W4VR1D3
3. into (out of) the glass
4. the void talks back
5. hope feels like a half chewed-liver
6. what's beyond the river
7. go back to where you came from
8. the puppet show
9. blood is for Ogun
10. new blood
11. ave imperator
12. kill or be killed
13. the importance of names
14. do not be afraid
15. old flame
16. subscription & mixed signals
17. queen
18. R3DFL4G
19. the hand you're dealt
20. white and black sunset
21. plastic rain
22. amateur arborist
23. run golgotha
24. trauma
25. happy birthday to the person who never celebrates
26. love is serious business

27. legacy
28. gimme some beauty
29. cannon, canon
30. N0FU3L
31. satellite voyeur
32. the slave master's advertisement
33. lacuna jammed/rolled away
34. city lights, goddamn
35. bushland blues '60
36. who's got your back?
37. the abomination
38. villain origin story
39. the only true (verify this) sacrament
40. xoxo
41. how fast can you go?
42. this is not wakanda
43. an idiot's guide
44. before/after god learnt to breathe fire
45. bridging distance
46. black protocol
47. 1885
48. and yet it remains blue
49. jumping ship
50. one last poem to take you home

1: WHAT EVEN IS HOME?

Home is the place, but it's also the face. The contradiction I carry through immigration, the question folded into cloth; Òrìṣà breathing softly in their respective colors, wrapped in ziplocks and bubble wrap innocuously labeled *religious items*, for scanners that cannot read spirit. And cannot see writ: bearing cores that were exiled from this soil, remade in sugarcane and saltwater, to be foreign while returning, to be the same but different... and so you ask yourself—*Will I be accepted? Will I be scorned? Will I be able to ignore the mockers and find community*… and dogs sniff for blood, but I have glamor'd my sacrifices with ground coffee, iron discipline and cowries kept close to the body where memory is warmest, so even when I hear the old insult snorted—*IJGB, you go wound o*—I just grab my rucksack. It's water off a duck's back. Aren't you reminded how impossible your own breath is? How statistical your survival feels, you whose ancestors were bent into open-air prisons as bloody non-entities in multiple dictatorships, but still arrived as people? I marvel at the madness of it, that I am here at all. I marvel at the madness of it.

2: W4VR1D3

Press your nose against the glass and see the future fog around your breath. Onisegun and world class centers for health, traffic conducted by Ògún's APIs, Òrìṣà Aje tilting crypto-market fluctuations with AI, *abbl.* My transport home is a silent mag-rail capsule. I remember when bedbugs were the apex predators of public transport, when I took a bus at Yaba, fresh from Port Harcourt and the engine refused resurrection until the driver performed exorcism by extraction, yanking out the entire dashboard clock: I remember the old thing buck—coughing to life only when chronology was disemboweled, order being merely a suggestion… but here I am, trip in progression, gliding in a vessel that carries me gently, like a compliant god, until we slow near my street and a cluster of supernatural police drift within few feet, grinning sheepishly, torchlights bouncing beams: [anything for the boys?] they ask. Palms are open, and the task, practised choreographed begging, and I wish thunder could give them a good pegging, because the uniforms have changed but the knavery has not. At last, I reach the address already half-cleansed by a patient housebot, dust negotiated into corners, and I step inside the nostalgia, drop my bags, I'm falling asleep fully clothed, telling myself I will rectify what needs rectifying tomorrow, as if tomorrow were not another deity with its own appetite.

3: INTO (OUT OF) THE GLASS

The coffee machine hums the rituals, and before my morning victuals, I wipe the cracked glass of the window where gremlins had hung film negatives, black eyes, and unused sedatives. Underwear of old lovers beside deja vu, dangle at an angle revealing my half-chewed liver; the sink gurgles a black river, and a small dragon lounges in the soap suds, arguing about taxes with Lei Gong on a unicycle. I recycle, then eat breakfast, feeding shadows on the wall. Of the world outside, these shadows rumble:

How badly do you have to fumble, for the Òrìṣà to
return in corporeal bodies to govern? How badly did
we mismanage our fire that the gods had to seize the
matches from our hands? Because we were given
lands and language and living knowledge and
somehow turned them into auction blocks again,
selling our attention, our future, our children's spine
to the highest bidder. How many times does a nation
forget before forgetting becomes a policy, how many
times do you kneel before you start calling the floor
your destiny?

The coffee hits. My brain is suddenly lit to the point where I can hear the city breathing. Drones greeting and delivering packages, small joys in the dark ages. In the news there's Zeus and the fresh crime his posse of death dealers have committed. The committee of thundergods internationale are putting out a statement to commiserate. I turn angrily to the mirror to remonstrate

And my eyes and memory disagree with what I am seeing. My reflection is peeing. Against the glass. I tell myself I must be dreaming still, but, alas… I am not. Perhaps there was something in the caf refill? I sneak a peak, just to be sure, and the mirror-me blinks when I do not. The knot in my stomach burns a hole that becomes a fright. Light's leaking out wrong, time's slurring out drunk, it reaches out and takes my wrist, and for some reason I don't resist. I obey and step into the glass.

Lei Gong—Thunder God of the Chinese. Often portrayed as an ugly beast. He might possess the body of a man but other features include a pair of wings, claws, and blue skin. He carries a mallet and drum seeking out wrong-doers His favourite instrument for punishment however, is the chisel.

4: THE VOID TALKS BACK

This is the badlands where they’re hunting down prophets,

hunting down ink

They’re hunting gangs and doppelgängers; they're making a stink.

In the eclipse, in this sudden darkness, birds stop singing,

spiders disassemble their webs, and the stinging

hornets disintegrate.

As consciousness is peeled away from vessel, silence

gets claustrophobic. Cliché echoes of [Why are we here?] permeate the fabric.

Floating golem in sentient space; in paradise, griots are

the nerfed version of seraphs that the trinity patched in update 3.3.8—

define blackness: resilience, atom to atom to molecule. Mí ò lè kú*. Cell to cell,

panting, planting, germinating

interrogating pollen like, if you are all good, how did

you harvest something as foul as the Satan?*

Yellow tape. This is a line you do not cross.

Yellow tape. This is a line you must not cross.

Mí ò lè kú—A Yoruba phrase literally meaning "I cannot die"

The satan—*the.* It's not a name, it's a title: the anti-everything-good, the adversary.

5: HOPE FEELS LIKE A HALF-CHEWED LIVER

Let me hypnotize you the old-fashioned way, book-walker

do not take your eyes off the line

do not take your eyes off the line

do not take your eyes off the line…

[Annnnd Sleep!]

When your feet tickle the scree, you begin to see

An oscillation of self, hanging high from lonesome rock

A rock baked in caked blood? *Blood.* A rock from which dark mysteries bud. *Bud.*

Below, a flood? Below, the mud?

Mud from whose belly you were formed. What's in *your* belly, child?

The sentence, the pain? The darkness you alone can touch,

in places unspoiled by torch? Can you fight manacles that do

not rust? How can faith be the one thing you do not trust? The eagle

screeches. See, tears are for bitches… you did the
crime, you do the

time flows below. Crashing, bashing, washing all;
drops

of red into vast river bed. The beak of the beast feasts
on

nerve and ink. Fire is a communicable disease. Avoid
being stuck on

dodecahedral memories in pleiadian theories—these
professors* should burn.

The further you go in our histories, the blacker the
Gods become. How

is a violent despair more muscular than hope? With
half-chewed liver

and vocal cords broken from screaming, the old titan
writhes in

open-eyed siesta. An oscillation of self, hanging high
from lonesome rock.

Do not take your eyes off the line.

Professors— German philosopher Hegel who declared 'Africa is no historical part of the world.' Hugh Trevor-Roper, Regius professor of History at Oxford University, who in 1963 openly expressed the racist view that Africa has no history. C.G. Seligman in his *Races of Africa*, who posited that Africans were incapable of achieving anything without Hamitic influence. The historian Niall Ferguson believes that colonial parliamentary democracy and the English language should be regarded as gifts to the colonized. Ferguson's views have been disseminated by television shows, by the way. A six-part series called Empire: How Britain Made the Modern World even aired on Channel 4. His works should burn.

Dodecahedron—A dodecahedron is any polyhedron with twelve flat faces. Armand Spitz used a dodecahedron as the "globe" equivalent for his Digital Dome planetarium projector based upon a suggestion from Albert Einstein.

Pleiadian theories—Rather than acknowledge the extraordinary feats of Africans, death dealers would rather credit ancient astronauts, extraterrestrials, or time travelers with Caucasian features as the original architects. A favourite target is the Pyramid of Giza. In 1979, Erich Von Däniken published a book called *Signs of the Gods?* where his racist views are boldly stated. In one of the chapters he asks "Was the black race a failure and did the extraterrestrials change the genetic code by gene surgery and then programme a white or a yellow race?"

6: WHAT'S BEYOND THE RIVER?

Grandma running circles around my dead father's electronic reincarnation

Her holographic dog barking

We repossessed Eden and sent the Cherubim packing

Mapped new algorithms for happiness

Wrote new codes for joy

Overhead, ads about memory upgrades hop in and out of sight

Dancing lights—here, you can share music by telepathy

Here, there are thirty strangers, in their heads, having a party

Hands link hands, link hands, link hands

Ambrosia from Ìyá Bàsírá's kitchen, is atop a 100,000 capacity skyscraper

Here, you can practically taste the laughter

Beyond the river, however, purist hunters still find species traitors

Refusing to master any tech smarter than smartphones

Last week, a man's shop was burnt down for trading
while being Igbo

Beyond the river, I guess nothing really changed.

7: GO BACK TO WHERE YOU CAME FROM

my reflection pulls me in and I smell lagoon salt and rust and the green breath of humus, as my feet leave terra firma, my life's replaying from obscene camera angles, borders screaming, [go back to where you came from!] at home I get the same words in vernacular, I'm like a chameleon that's lost its blender. my back scrapes thorns, blood blooms ceremonial and bright, because of my fair skin. [which tribe are you?] the corridor ahead is wet verdant light, vines gossiping, statues blinking, spirits updating their software, and the reflection speaks without moving its mouth, the voice is mine played backward through a cracked speaker, saying: down | saying: where they keep the teeth | saying: fear is only memory learning how to hunt, and when the mirror seals behind us with the sound of a song ending too soon, I suddenly understand how doubt and devotion share a spine, how home is a frequency, not just a place, how my body, seven octillion atoms trembling, had been tuned for this descent all along.

8: THE PUPPET SHOW

Ladies & gentlemen! Welcome to the dystopia

This is plenty, this is cruise, this is cornucopia

I come to, like a rebooted machine dumped back into meat, my eyes open against a ceiling of cages, the rage is the hysteric light, testosterone thick as incense, sweat, piss and shite (human and fowl, alike) fermenting into a warm jeer; my tongue tastes iron and warm tear, and the arena breathes me in, it is a lung made of concrete and neon, feathers glued to blood, boots skidding in mud, roosters losing their minds in the rafters, slashing at each other with razor blades attached to their spurs; I lay there counting my bones while bets are shouted in gold and DigiCoins. The rules are cruel, and can be compressed into one: make your death entertaining.

There is a puppet-show before the main event

& a cute showrunner, cherubic, effervescent

I watch from the ring with my knuckles sweating [god abeg] as a cyberpunk shrine unfolds in front of us—strings, shadows wearing voices, and a live dog actor. The common factor: famine, everyone starving. But the dog stayed alive, the sleek pooch with secrets, a tortoise heavy with questions, coaxing, cajoling; until the dog, cornered into confession, said it was her mother in the sky who fed her. The tortoise begged to follow, so they went to the bush where a tree grew taller than eyes had yet seen, and the dog sang: [mother, mother, please let down your rope!] and the sky answered with a ladder falling mercifully; the dog climbing first, the tortoise close behind, my heart climbing with them, my ribs clicking like the puppets' joints; at the top, a door opened into abundance, bowls of food, freshest palmwine, the mother old and blind, hugging her child for the memories, and when they returned to the forest floor they parted, satisfied.

But not for long. Not for long. For longer-throat is a powerful sickness, and the tortoise practicing alone; sang the song again, a counterfeit larynx wearing the dog's voice, hurrying the blind mother so she wouldn't feel the lie in her hands, stuffing his shell with too much future, descending fast, gravity aiding and abetting; the dog, serendipitously, saw and screamed: [mother, mother, cut the rope!] and the mother, waking to betrayal, severed the link, and the tortoise fell through light and crashed, shell shattering into lessons… *etc, etc.*

> the crowd laughs and hisses, the cute host grinning begins one of his speeches, his voice buttered with menace, and midway through begins the glitches—his face stuttering, jaw snapping, eyes desyncing from smiles—as if

the story had ruptured inside like piles, but he recovers, wipes sweat, bows to applause, and there may have been one more song: of angelic puppeteers who themselves are being puppeteered… but he did not play it.

9: BLOOD IS FOR OGUN

The man next to me laughs at my naïveté, until a betting cock (thrown or freed, idk) becomes a feathered missile, clips a light, spirals, and slits his throat mid-lunge, the universe refuses to apologize as red sprays [Blood is for Ogun always.] and the crowd howls approval, odds adjusting; somewhere above, the reflection laughs, pleased, and a man's lunging, air splitting where my head had been, I roll in sus-dust, coughing dark oaths, the dog jumps into the fray, clamping an arm—and I move on instinct learned from a life of fleeing, sidestep, elbow, knee, letting rage trip over itself, refusing the final note; music seeps in, breath finding tempo, and I listen, slipping between strikes, redirecting momentum, a shaitan behind my ear asking why I wouldn't kill and me answering that I do not belong to this song, the crowd booing, debris hissing on impact, the arena shrinking, hungrier, the dog barking me out of a blade meant for my spine, a counter knocking metal free, a fall cracking skull on stone, silence rippling then applause, and me standing amid wreckage while screen recalculates and the cherubic Showrunner jubilates, mouth full of jagged teeth, calling it interesting that I survived without becoming ugly…

10: NEW BLOOD

Ding-ding-ding!

… and shadows are herded out from cages: whole neighborhoods extracted from trucks. Mothers, dancers, accountants, children, all inventory; faces multiply, overlap, strangers wearing my eyes, my eyes wearing theirs, everyone reflected and therefore complicit, because to watch is to feed, and the arena feeds on attention, feeds on blindness donning the cap of banter, and I see the populace picked at: selected/discarded blood is refracted into applause, prayers buffered, delayed, and dropped. The cute death dealer adjusts his glasses in the reflection though he has no eyes there, only sockets glowing with metrics, engagement rates, thunder-god satisfaction indexes, terrified of another glitch. *Everybody knows what happened to the last person to hold this position.* And I try to step away but the mirror follows, stretches, becomes floor, becomes ceiling, becomes the skin on my hands…

11: AVE IMPERATOR

[We who are about to die salute you!] The world is drunken cheers, mouth odor and the rearing of sunken fears. Right in front of me is this colossus with his chrome-veined shoulder and a cybernetic leg bzzt-bzzing with servo-hunger, there is a reed-thin knife of a man whose reach must be at least 80 inches in span, the stocky bruiser tattooed in rainbow ink, the bald giant covered in eczema and stink, there's a pacing acrobat wired with subdermal LEDs, and the last, already trembling, I think may be on MEDs, whose pupils roll back as Kure mounts him, the Hyena-spirit snapping at musicians, drool threading from his grin while an attendant clutches the leash of his rage lest the audience suffer accidental injury. The kalangu begins to speak in pitch-bent prophecy, squeezing and releasing its thongs until Hausa panegyrics leap from goatskin:

> Dan taguwa da saurin girma! the drum cries in high-low arcs; *—young he-camel, fast-growing;* Dawan da kututturai; dawan da mala'iku!*—jungle of stumps, jungle of angels of death*; Dawo Audu ci bayi; mai horo da masaba!*—return, capturer of slaves, blacksmith's hammer;* Duna na Sakkwato…

The drums recall each man into being, swell their heads and then we collide. I become water as the great teacher said, slipping between concussions, letting gravity collect its debts from others: the chrome-shouldered titan loses his prosthetic in a grapple and it becomes a cudgel, swung against his own skull until sparks burst; the reed-man screams as thumbs find his eyes and the arena goes red and blind; the rainbow chest caves under a knee and he spits blood like a busted hydrant; the bald giant is kissed in the temple with an Aluwo charm and slumps as the juju unplugs him; Kure's hyena-mouth lunges and is yanked back, escorted out still snarling. I am water, my friend, water; I survive by accident and nimbleness while they do the heavy lifting of ruin, and when the last man turns toward me, the drum speaks again… [we who are about to die salute you!] Aut non.

Among the 'yam bori, the act of possession by a spirit involves the loss of the devotee's sense. The devotee is referred to as a "mare" (godiya) or, if a male, a "horse" (doki), which the spirits ride in a similar fashion to how one "mounts" a partner in the act of sexual intercourse.

12: KILL OR BE KILLED

He comes at me, elephant musth, all reinforced deltoids and sponsored fury, his fists are demolition maces, and my size can't tie his laces; so I sidestep the headline of his punch and answer with a precise low kick that tests the peroneal nerve and turns his thunder into static, timing over speed, hinge over hammer; he swings again and I slip inside the arc, feel the wind of it shear a strand of hair, and drive two knuckles into the soft switch beneath his ear where balance goes to die, the crowd's volume, my guy, is as if someone toggled the sky; he roars and bull-rushes, so I give him air, pivot on the ball of my foot and let his mass draft clear, then lace an elbow into the floating ribs: once, twice, and when he hooks wild I intercept the wrist, torque it into a brief, bright geometry, step behind him and scissor his ankle while my forearm scythes across his throat; he stumbles, the arena floor rumbles: a verdict, a verdict, and I harvest the moment: precision over power… heel snapping into the solar plexus, a calibrated detonation that empties him, then a final, small, nail on the coffin, strike to the noggin where thought fizzles out; he goes down in slow code, grilled teeth clacking, blood mapping a mess across the mat. I'm sat, and I can see my reflection cupped in his glazing eyes, it's pixelated by pain, and this version of me is vain; it smiles and says [now you can no longer say you're innocent,] and the kalangu tightens its thongs and answers in high-low breath… *you have won a million DigiCoins, your life is about to change!!!* Which is when I knew the danger had only just learned my name…

13: THE IMPORTANCE OF NAMES

My old man taught me how to make weapons from fine sand*

Ọrúnmìlà baba ifa

My old man taught me how to shake the thundergod's hand

Ọrúnmìlà baba ifa

My old man witnessed a thousand melanated sons
cleaned out from history books

Ọrúnmìlà baba ifa

My old man also witnessed the mutilation of looks

Ọrúnmìlà baba ifa

My old man taught me the finer points of mind games

Ọrúnmìlà baba ifa

My old man taught me to choose my own names...

Ọrúnmìlà—

Oh, and to live up to them!

I dance joyously, as you should too, my child

away from baptists who try to drown you for their own sins

The cattle egret that takes flight from atop the opoto tree, then perches on top of the lime tree,

It gains a lot of wisdom in the process.

Fine sand— As early as 1864, similarities had been noted between the Dahomean Fa and the "geomancy of the Greeks", also practiced by the Arabs under the name of Al-Raml, 'The sand,' because the figures were cast upon the desert floor. Napoleon brought back to Europe a manuscript found in upper Egypt which contained some of the secrets. His "Book of Fate" is a notable specimen of European and modern vulgarization. Dahomean Fa and Yoruba Ifa are neighbours, sand-cutting is practiced by Muslim alfas.

Ọrúnmìlà— father of Ifa and all the odù

Baptists—In the old days, Africans were denied access to health care, education and other amenities we regard as basic today, unless they could prove they were baptized and were given a Christian name. Some of the names stuck and have become legacy family names.

opoto—fig tree.

14: DO NOT BE AFRAID

[I am Gabriel, I am beautiful, I am strong, I am forged of trumpet-blast and clean fire, I am not afraid of this animal called man, with his terrible decision-making and infinite capacity to be foolish when spooked… do not be afraid.]

I imagine that this self-affirmation is not for us, but for the archangel, because look around, all we have are frightened leaders wrapped in medals and tin-foil armor, scared of glitches, scared of losing their access, and fear makes them inventive, fear builds cages, fear sharpens laws into knives, fear would rather plunge the world into a curated hell than loosen its grip for a single honest second, and I stand there, newly crowned champion, sweat drying into salt maps across my chest, the crowd's roaring, cheering, and the cute showrunner leans forward with teeth like spikes on a cemetery gate and says [make a wish], as per I have stumbled into a fairy tale sponsored by jinns, and I say I wish that all the bloodletting will end, because I really just want to go home, and he laughs, [very well], he says, [very well, get our champion new clothes, food and drink], and the crowd applauds once more, bloated, while elsewhere knives are simultaneously being washed and sharpened, and I understand then what the angel sees…

15: OLD FLAME

Memory has torn a hole through the present and stepped out wearing her old denim jacket with the frayed cuff she used to worry between her fingers when she lied about being fine,

She was gorgeous, and our eyes lock and the world does not stop but it warps around the axis of that gaze, and suddenly I am in a daze, no longer spectacle, I am the boy who knew the scent of coconut oil and conditioner in her hair, the way it clung to my pillow… [you work here?[

I hear the exact pitch of her laugh: three rising notes and a snort she tried to swallow—see the chipped blue polish on her left thumb, the spray of freckles on her nose, all of it rushes me at once, a flood without mercy, while blood dries on my knuckles and the crowd chants my name

and she looks at me, at the red soaking my shirt, the split skin, the animal breath heaving in my chest, and her mouth trembles with grief, and she says, [oh gods above, what has the world turned you into?] and I want to tell her everything, how it peeled me, how it auctioned the softer parts, but the words dissolve before reaching my tongue, because in her eyes I see that she knows. I was built for verses and loops and staying small, not this cut-throat hustle...

16: SUBSCRIPTION & MIXED SIGNAL

Eat, this is my body, and do not flinch at the bone, for while it feels forbidden it is filling, the pulse of stars fermented into flesh. In the marrow, taste the echo of centuries, the sigh of prophets kneeling on dust, the laughter of saints forgotten by time. Do this in remembrance of me, and remember that the knife that cleaves the loaf cleaves the soul, that the bread is life and the hymn is a riot song, and the table folds into your lap like a sky upside down. Swallow, and know that the divine is neither far nor near but trembling in your teeth, that to eat is to become the feast…

Drink, this is my blood. Drink, and feel it surge like lightning through the veins. The cup spilling galaxies into your mouth, into your esophagus, into the synapses where memory deconstructs and reconstitutes… Sip slowly, till the river within you remembers its source; map of all journeys, all wars, all lullabies ever sung under the crescent sky. Drink, book-walker, and your tongue will taste the sigh of oceans. Drink, and know what it is to commune with the unsayable, to swallow the sacred paradox, to sip the chaos distilled into order, to tremble with joy that is almost unbearable. Do this in remembrance of me.

17: QUEEN

Oh, she is black & augmented, sexy & confident.
four things they don't want to be seen

she is hot & vibrant, is anti-fragile,
and they all love the gossamer fabric on
her skin.

but in every newsfeed, there are all these suitors
blaming her for their own sin.
they are targeting her kin & canceling her being.
allegedly.
the first time they hit her, she turned the other cheek,
the second time it happened, she said [pass the
ammo]
allegedly.

her name's changed so many times, but
what I remember is: we, sitting in the sunset
holding hands, & duiker-watching. she
had this pretty dress on, sequins in sequence
I put a rose petal in her hair
& she shook it out
she seemed so mad that the camera only worked in
sepia* out here. I'll take the blue skies, any day.
the lush green fields, & frolic in the clear water.
she was
melodic moments merging magic & miracles
her only crime being that she grew up fast.
hips, first, full-of-riddles
lips, too, singing with the fiddles

soft spoken, yet laughing out loud
camwood culture, cursive eyelashes, I do not recognize the
tattooed smiles covering up these tear stains now.
they say time heals all wounds—they also say black don't crack;
why should I take self-fetishization seriously,
when I've seen her broken in ways no one should break? she
said [pass the (ammo) dreams, dimples & damage]
said [re-engineer the outrage] sweet, saturated soil
for pyrophtes… she said [pass, te amo] this is home, re-cultivated
                                        for love.

this is home, navel of the rainbow.
and if you haven't yet figured it out
the woman I've been speaking about
is Afruika.

Afruika— Gerald Massey, in 1881, stated that Africa is derived from the Egyptian af-rui-ka, meaning "to turn toward the opening of the Ka." The Ka is the energetic double of every person and the "opening of the Ka" refers to a womb or birthplace. Africa would be, for the Egyptians, "the birthplace." There are some who say the original name for the continent is Alkebulan, which is translated as "mother of mankind," or "the garden of Eden." Alkebulan is an extremely old word, and, even though it sounds like Arabic, its origins are indigenous. Apparently, many nations in Africa used this word, including the Ethiopians, Nubians, Moors, and Numidians.

Turning the other cheek— is often misinterpreted. It was an act of defiance to force a person to smack you with an open palm instead of backhanded. In the New Testament, one could hit people of equal social stature with an open hand, but could only backhand those socioeconomically lower.

Sepia— Hollywood directors habitually use the same yellow palette to dramatize stories taking place in Africa, Latin America and South Asia. The official reason is to cast these places as universally hot, dry and dusty. Unofficially, however, it is quite simply a third world aesthetic; a way to make viewers associate it with poverty and lawlessness. Some filmmakers argue it is not that deep; it is just to create a feeling of tension and action. But why is this not applied to U.S based action films? Meanwhile, blue is the exact opposite of the yellow, representing futuristic, vibrant and progressive societies.

18: R3DFL4G

She takes my hand as though obeying the showrunner's decree, and leads me behind the neon marquee and she hugs me with such fierceness, whispers into my blood-matted collar that we have to flee, because she thinks, those words, [give him new clothes, food and drinks] were not rewards to be paid, but code, soft syllables lacquered over a blade, [no one wins against the house,] she says, they harvest their champions like seasonal fruit, their messiahs are limited editions, they turn their faces into memes, salt their names until history cannot swallow them, and I'm thinking [conspiracy?] but her eyes are already scanning for unmanned gates, and she drags me into the garage where the showrunner's car waits, low and predatory, humming with illegal firmware and a dashboard itching to go, and I reach for the wires beneath the steering column, but my fingers hesitate, because this is not a Hollywood movie where protagonists are fluent in heroics and escape, I do not know how to hotwire destiny, and it embarrasses me; so she exhales, gently displaces me, and peels back the panel with the calm of someone who has rehearsed survival in secret, twists copper nerves together and the engine purrs awake, and the conspirator dog from the show comes bounding in, and we drive toward the thin, improbable seam where choice still battles against the script.

19: THE HAND YOU'RE DEALT

♧

I felt it before I knew it, a tightening in the air like the intake before a scream, and then the chase began furious and extreme—engines multiplying, urban combat utility vehicles, cruisers, pods spilling from hidden ramps and vine-choked hideaways the way cockroaches scatter when you lift a rotten plank, their headlights going jskghjskgh, their hulls mismatched, scavenged, hungry, drones peeling off into the canopy like metallic mosquitoes with red eyes, and somewhere a horn blew diabolical, ancient and digital at once, announcing centaurs bursting from the underbrush, half-flesh half-machine, torsos welded to luminous haunches, hooves striking sparks from stone as they galloped…

♡

My old flame chortled and punched the throttle, the car answered with a roar that vibrated my teeth into percussion. The chassis rode high on adaptive magnetic suspension, adrenaline into a drum solo, dog braced herself between seats, eyes engaged, and the road fractured into choices too fast to regret—the front end was fitted with a brush-cutter grille and articulated ram bars, roots snapping, water spraying,

HUD screaming probabilities, drone clipped branch and pinwheeled into a tree, a blossom of sparks. Another fired acid that grazed our tail and dissolved against the shields with a hiss like a disappointed snake, a jake centaur leapt alongside us, close enough for me to see the human fear stitched into his jaw beneath the luster and bravado, and I shouted something I didn't plan

words tearing free because fear makes you do things, the music of physics kicking in, tempo, drop, acceleration: my heart syncing with the engine, overstimulation, the car skidding sideways across mud slick with algae and old blood, my old flame threading gaps no map would admit existed, trees bending like they recognized her, cockroach car piling up behind in a clatter of ego and metal, one flipping end over end, another exploding beautifully, drones swarming, centaurs firing, and the jungle answering with fog and thorns and sudden turns, and through it all the lagoon smell grew louder, salt and promise cutting through exhaust, and I thank Ògún the path-clearer. Tell me why he laughs at *my* unbelief in myself. [Sometimes,] he says [survival is nothing mystical at all, just momentum arguing with fate at very high volume.]

20: WHITE AND BLACK SUNSET

We are
Moving at the speed of light, the speed of life,
cutting like the sleek of knife through butter on
deserted highway. Some super-mega hit is receiving
air play and the world is golden with the setting sun.
It's the perfect time to take a selfie, son—
Until, out of nowhere, a group of gazelle fawn
appear in single file, crossing the road.
Fulcrum and load, Ògún can fold the metal for
cushion, but he doesn't. To teach a new lesson, he
disappears.

You must learn to control your affairs.
The whole world revolves in black
and white, spinning
clear of the kaleidoscope of sunset.

Ah Nubian majesty, just look at us, stepping out the

debris—dust and smoke like Tetris

We are

Unscathed and thankful; looking forward to going
back home

mildly bewildered like, [what the hell is all this
monochrome?]

But then the camera cuts to acid rain and the dodo
and

the quagga and white rhino*

frolicking yonder in knee-high grass... then you get it.

The dodo— The last widely accepted sighting of a dodo was in 1662.

The quagga was distinguished from other zebras by its limited pattern of primarily brown and white stripes, mainly on the front part of the body. The rear was brown and without stripes, and appeared more horse-like. They were once found in great numbers in the Karoo of Cape Province and the southern part of the Orange Free State in South Africa. After the European settlement of South Africa began, the quagga was extensively hunted, as it competed with domesticated animals for forage.

Some were taken to zoos in Europe, but breeding programmes were unsuccessful. The last wild population lived in the Orange Free State; the quagga was extinct in the wild by 1878. The last captive specimen died in Amsterdam on 12 August 1883. Only one quagga was ever photographed alive, and only 23 skins exist today.

the white rhino— Sudan, the world's last known male northern white rhinoceros, died in Kenya on 19 March 2018.

21: PLASTIC RAIN

fat drops of god-tear
land on my forehead,
all birds that drink it are winding up dead

fat drops in flow-stream,
fat drops in bloodstream
all truths that drink it are winding up dead.

Researchers find that over 1,000 metric tons of microplastic particles fall into 11 protected areas in the western US each year. Imagine how many metric tons fall into Nigeria! That's the equivalent of over 120 million plastic water bottles. Mind you, the 'protected areas in the West', accounts for only 6 percent of the total US area.

Plastic rain looks like it's going to be a more sinister conundrum than acid rain. (Acid rain is the result of sulfur dioxide and nitrogen oxide emission, by the way). By deploying scrubbers in power plants to control the former, and catalytic converters in cars to control the latter, many 'first world' countries have been able to cut down on the acidification challenge. And microplastic? That's a different beast altogether. The hardiness makes it seemingly impossible to eradicate. And guess what?

Plastic waste is expected to skyrocket from 260 million tons a year to 460 million tons by 2030.

all the truths—Big corporations pointing fat fingers at small scale individual footprints. The same fossil fuel and plastics the corporations used to develop their countries have suddenly become destructive to a continent with the least emissions. Are you trying to stop climate change or the development of Africa?

22: AMATEUR ARBORIST

The mortar used for pounding yams will not do for
pounding indigo leaves;

The mortar for pounding indigo leaves will not do for
yams;

The tray on which beads are displayed for sale will
not do for displaying dried okro

Pangaea-old trees do not stand amused by irreverent
axe

First, amateur arborist,

You must ask yourself, how am I the apex predator?

Your mother's body resides inside the belly of an
Àràbà*

We take your Carbon dioxide and give you our waste

We cultivate you for nitrogen and your inhumation is
a feast

Pangaea-old trees do not stand amused by irreverent
axe

The overreaching mud idol that asked to be put in the
rain:

As the arms fell off, so did the thighs

The rounded head could not support itself.

Àràbà—Kapok tree.

23: RUN GOLGOTHA

they tried to lynch God

strung him up on burning cross

but Ọba Kòso.

Ọba Kòso— this refers to the story where Ṣàngó, heartbroken and banished from his own kingdom, purportedly commits suicide by hanging. His worshippers disprove this, saying he ascended to the heavens instead. 'Ọba Kòso' literally means 'the king did not hang'. It forms a parallel with the story of the resurrected Christ.

24: TRAUMA

Shittiest luck to have the lead bully as your guardian./ I learned early that the sucker's love/ came with heavy hands, every/ insult as ellipses chaining one doubt to the next,/ and in that house my name was shortened/ into something easier to shout,/ easier to bruise, until self-esteem leaked out/ and nobody noticed the dark growing thicker;

he trained me in smallness: heat and strike, heat and strike, telling me

I was lazy when I rested, stupid when I asked why, arrogant when I dreamed,

and soon his voice was renting space behind my eyes.

I remember staring at my reflection/ in a sitting room's mirror,/ asking myself why do I need to be great,/ why is goodness not enough?/ Why is kindness treated like a defect,/ a soft spot for the world to poke until it bleeds./ He said greatness was survival, that only the loud and sharp eat,/ that the rest become soup,/ and I swallowed it because children swallow whatever is put in their mouths,/ even poison wrapped in proverbs.

So when you found me, my darling, every failure was feeling like

confirmation that   he was right,   that I was a
misprint, a draft   that should have been   discarded,
and even now

when praise comes, it feels like a trick coin
that will vanish if I touch it too hard.

I still find myself wondering if my worth/ could exist without an audience,/ without blood on the floor to prove I fought for it./ I am still that child sometimes, flinching/ at footsteps, negotiating with my own/ ambition, trying to believe/ that being kind is not the same as being weak,/ that surviving him was already an act of greatness,   even if   no one   clapped.

25: HAPPY BIRTHDAY TO THE PERSON WHO NEVER CELEBRATES

No cake has ever learned your name.
No knife has cut a slice for you.
You have blown out nothing—

But your heart *knows* how many times it has survived.
And life keeps count even when you refuse to
And your liver knows how many wars it has fought
And life keeps count even when you refuse to

So, have your introspection. Be solemn. Make no wish
if wishing feels like bargaining with unreliable gods,
Because I already made one for you:
the sky split open in glorious chiaroscuro,
time licking sugar from your fingers,
your name written quickly in light
before the wind edits it.

Eat the day slowly. Let joy sit beside you without explanation.

Allow yourself to be acknowledged by the ancestor that keeps insisting on you.

Allow yourself to enjoy the universe's choicest blessings!

Allow yourself.

26: LOVE IS SERIOUS BUSINESS

The city warped as it usually did every time I said [I love you.] Love you in the buses floating like black and yellow whales. Love you as the streetlamps sing neon oriki. Love you like this is the miracle of the alley bazaar, where hackers sell shady salvations/patches that erase guilt, and I told you stories instead of buying dinner, fed you laughter. Every past lover's voice lived in my chest: [love must earn its keep] affection - provision = noise, etc. but you leaned into my empty hands like they were enough, like my presence was enough. And that terrified me.

In that season, romance was a mangled thing. My insecurities crawled out, ugly, vicious, driving you to tears. I kept rehearsing a gesture big enough to drown my doubt. Big enough to repeat the way your eyes lit up, when I had saved enough to buy the boots you liked.

But disappearance is better than disappointment, and I convinced myself you deserved someone fully assembled, someone with receipts for their self-worth, someone whose pockets didn't echo when you asked for tomorrow. The city warped one last time: goodbye splashed as rain falling upward, my footsteps erasing themselves, your name = fading neon sign. . . I left because I couldn't believe love would stay.

27: LEGACY

Onwuchuruba [only death stops me from being
wealthy]; And I can still hear the songs, *Nna ha-tanu*
oji, ihe ayi nacho bu ndu—

ancestors eat kola, what we ask is life, and I honor that river, I honor the lineage branching like palm fronds insisting on tomorrow, all these while I stand at its bank and confess a heresy—I do not want children… and the village wind tilts its head as if I have refused oxygen, as if I have spat into continuity. What on earth is wrong with you?

onye di ndu odikwute ihe, he who is alive will stumble on good fortune, and good fortune is spelled with sons who keep the tree from withering, but what if my stewardship of *ndu* is ~~replication~~ restraint, ~~multiplication~~ attention, what if I have watched too many men demand puppies of the future with the impatience of boys, cooing at the idea of legacy while someone else will wake for the crying, clean the mess, mortgage the marrow, and I have seen women conscripted, barely hiding resentment, seen men who do not want children branded selfish, less than, unfinished, because masculinity is a factory whose only acceptable product is offspring, and I refuse that arithmetic, because I am not joining you people to gamble another consciousness against a world already frayed, and if *ndu* is endless, if continuation is a mystery beyond the grave, then perhaps my offering is honesty, a couple decades of deliberate living, a branch that chooses not to branch, and that too is life, and it is not a crime.

28: GIMME SOME BEAUTY

with the engine humming softer now, its own way of saying speed attracts ghosts, and the jungle opened into something so lush it felt obscene, a shrine built by a god with no sense of restraint, colors overfed and dripping: euphonias bursting from branches like living jewels, reed warblers stitching the air with silver thread-song, yellow-breasted boubous calling flirtatious insults, pheasants strutting through clearings in impossible robes, blues and copper and rot, sound is a surplus resource here, and the flowers—God—the flowers were just showing off, purples so deep they bruised the eyes, whites too clean for a world that knew blood, Iroko trees that had outlived empires, and the perfume was thick and sweet and decaying at once. See, the beauty turned up past comfort until it curdled, until it made my stomach twist, because I could feel how easily such abundance could swallow you whole, and we slowed, listening for engines that never came, only the click of insects conducting meetings in the undergrowth, the drip of water negotiating gravity, the dog standing alert in the back seat, nose high, reading stories written in scent, [nothing] and I felt my body finally notice itself again, small tremors, skin tight with dried sweat, blood cooling from its earlier riot…

and for a moment, this griot wanted to stop completely, to step out and let the green claim me, to become another story the jungle tells itself when it rains, but the sick beauty warned me, low tones through pollen, that staying is also a kind of death, and the mothers arcane* warned me, that the same lushness that heals can erase, and so we kept moving, slow and deliberate, leaving only bent grass and displaced air behind us, putting kilometers and histories and the cute deathdealer's hunger, between us and thanking the olu'gbo while the bushes close gently after us like it had never seen a thing.

Mothers Arcane—or Iyaami Oshorounga. According to a legend from Òsá Méjì, when the primordial beings and deities descended from the spiritual realm to inhabit the Earth, Ìyáàmi was unable to join them because she was entirely naked. Feeling excluded, she appealed to the other beings for assistance, but none responded to her plea. Eventually, she approached Òrúnmìlà, who understood her true nature and character, and asked him to help her descend to the Earth. Òrúnmìlà questioned how she intended to travel in her naked state. In response, Ìyáàmi assured him that if he permitted her, she wouldllenter unseen, so that no one would perceive her presence. Convinced, Òrúnmìlà agreed to assist her.

However, upon their arrival on Earth, Òrúnmìlà requested that Ìyáàmi depart from him as agreed. She refused. When he warned that she might starve if she remained, she ominously declared that she would instead consume him from within. Alarmed by this threat, Òrúnmìlà consulted the Ifá oracle through divination. Guided by the revealed odu, he performed the prescribed sacrifices and made offerings specifically to appease Ìyáàmi. When she perceived and accepted the sacrifice, she was satisfied, and Òrúnmìlà took the opportunity to leave.

From that moment, the power of Ìyáàmi became firmly established on Earth. She and her companions settled within the forest, where they selected particular trees to serve as their sacred abodes and instruments of influence. Some of these trees were designated for benevolent purposes, while others were associated with malevolent forces. Among them were orogbo, iroko, arere, ose, obobo, iya, and asurin.

29: CANNON, CANON*

To the master of instruments in Lagoon Town—

[steal*], said the Bible thumper.* [steal]
[kill], said the guinea* stomper [kill]
we stammer our way through ombuds jargons,
paddling our own canoes, & wheeling our wagons

this lagoon once flowed with life and grace,
a nurturing, bountiful gentle place.
but evil clowns made their evil way down,
& all the joy was replaced with pain & disgrace

first, all that water turned to blood,
a crimson gush, a sign of god.
the big fish died, the crops all failed,
the cops who shoulda done something? the suckers bailed

next came the thug-frogs, in endless throngs,

they filled the streets with so many wrongs.
the gnats & flies and termites came,
& all the land was filled with shame.

the hail & fire that fell from sky,
destroyed the banks & made men cry.
the locusts came & ate the rest,
the brain drain took the very best

the darkness came, a-thick, & deep,
& all the land was made to weep.
the death of firstborn, was a final blow,
but bats hid their spawn in foreign snow.

the lagoon's plague's a bitter tale,
of suffering, of death, of woe and wail.
but also of a powerful god,
whose will and skill-set will always be odd.

Cannon, Canon– Many of the castles slave traders built on the coasts of West Africa were guarded with cannons. Elmina Castle in Ghana is one of such. It was built in 1482 by the Portuguese, but taken over by the Dutch in 1637. They built a Reformed church close to the Governor's quarters. Over its entrance is a plaque which says "God resides in this place". God did not reside in the female slaves' dungeons below, though. The governor, from his entrance hall, would watch enslaved African women as they were paraded through the small courtyard. Any woman who took his fancy was summoned to his quarters. Those who refused were chained to a cannonball to be cooked in the sun in the main square. The other European guards, following the Guv's lead, got to rape whichever slave caught their fancy.

Steal— in 1899, Henry Labouchère, the MP for Middlesex, described the process by which territory was acquired for the British Empire during a parliamentary meeting. "Someone belonging to one company or another meets a black man. Of course, he has an interpreter with him. He asks the black man if he is the proprietor of a certain land, and if he will sign a paper, he shall have a bottle of gin. The black man at once accepts; a paper is put before him, and he is told to make his mark on it, which he does. And then we say that we have made a treaty by which all the rights in that country of the emperor, king, or chief, or whatever you call him, have been given over to us. That is the origin of all these treaties."

"If the negroes be generally crafty and treacherous, it may well be said the Europeans have not dealt with them as becomes Christians, for it is too well known that many of the European nations trading amongst these people have very unjustly and inhumanly, without any provocation, stolen away from time to time abundance of the people, not only in this coast, but all over **Guinea**, and when they came on board their ships in a harmless and confiding manner, carried great numbers away to the plantations..."

– Jean Barbot (1679)

Bible thumper— According to Flora Shaw (British journalist and the annoying woman who allegedly gave Nigeria its name) "The Portuguese had consistently sent many Catholic missionaries among the natives of the coast, and then, as now, *commerce and conversion* went hand in hand." Mission work is inextricably and inherently colonial in nature, and has resulted in the devastation of indigenous peoples around the globe, and is at the root of countless cultural genocides.

Guinea is an old word for the people of West Africa. In Berber tongue—*ghinawen*, it meant 'the burnt people'. Based on their complexion alone, they were treated as subhuman by both Arabs and Europeans. In America, many 'burnt people' were actually burnt to death by their masters who were always quoting Ephesians 6:1.

30: N0FU3L

I stared at the dead console blinking red. The car itself had turned witness against me, and I thought, absurdly, perhaps if escape didn't still require fuel refined from old violence, perhaps if we had chosen a ride with solar panels… then I heard him, cherubic death dealer, approaching in colonizer confidence, convoy winking into existence, charms fully funded, engines purring, drones hovering, laughter telling of shortcuts and administrative magomago, the sound of a man who believes he can do and undo

•

And rage rose in me: sedimentary + layered across a hundred years of harm, and my lover held my arm: I know I am not free, and it makes me so angry, angry in a way that has no choreography, angry like a field remembering chains long after they rusted away. Centuries after slavery my people are still enslaved culturally, taught to apologize to mirrors that do not reflect us, feeling inferior by curriculum, economically dependent like children punished into gratitude, psychologically conditioned to chase dopamine crumbs scattered so we forget to ask who owns the bakery, spiritually stunted by imported heavens that rent space in our very dreams, communally redesigned to feed a greedy mammon-moloch system that eats children, and drinks their blood. This is the root of my rage, and the way the engine dying felt scripted, like history repeating because nobody changed the fuel source.

31: SATELLITE VOYEUR

The end-result of

Space-age programming & ancient cryptography

250 random odù*,

9 billion permutations & combinations

A,C,T,G married to cascading raw codes

in whorls of your palms & in the mind's telescope.

There's free-will that you will pay for, baked into
binary palindrome

Every frame of mind, every film frame of life

ad infinitum.

Big brother is watching

And one does not speak the name of God in vain.

Satellite voyeur?

No, it does not worry me that Òrìṣà watches me
déshabillé

What worries me is that Òrìṣà can see disaster
looming

And she does nothing.

Odù—Patterns of binary code, opened and closed nodules which represent all the energies enclosed in Igba Iwa, the calabash of existence /universe.

lfa is a system of divination based on sixteen basic and 256 derivative figures obtained either by the manipulation of sixteen palm nuts, or by the toss of a chain of eight half seed shells.

32: THE SLAVE MASTER'S ADVERTISEMENT

Yesterday

Needed: Natives in their mid-20s

Who have had chicken pox* before and survived;

strong mitochondria, not prone to deicide

Broad chested or else with well-rounded buttocks, fertile*.

caesalpinia* prohibited onboard.

[Why would you eat the Pride of Barbados?* Why?]

Today

Needed: The best brains, the best black,

the least woke, the most jack—premium teeth for smiling,

able to abet industrial scale

entertainment, experiment, exploitation and engineering

of God

For mirrors and salt?*

Insults and insults and still, like you

I apply.

Who have had chickenpox—enslaved people who had had chicken pox were thought to be more valuable than those who had not because then they were immune to a new attack and chicken pox was a serious, fatal problem in those days. More sinisterly, those who had survived were farmed for their genes and experimented upon. In smallpox vaccine development, enslaved infants were literally infected with this virus and the ooze their bodies produced was used as vaccine matter.

Fertile— To fully appreciate the devilishness of medical racism, you need to read the autobiography of J.Marion Sims "The father of Modern Gynecology" and see how, in the 1800s, he experimented on Black women (without anesthesia, because 'Black women do not feel pain').

Caesalpinia—a species of flowering plant in the pea family. All caesalpinia are poisonous. The immature seeds of some are edible however, after roasting.

Pride of Barbados—a nickname for caesalpinia. In the 17th century, Maria Sibylla Merian wrote in her work Metamorphosis insectorum Surinamenisum: "The slaves who are not treated well by their Dutch masters, use the seeds of this plant to abort their children, so their children will not become slaves like they are. Black slaves from Guinea and Angola have demanded to be well treated, threatening to refuse to have children. They told me this themselves."

Mirrors, salt—(add gin and umbrellas to that list) this is the defense racist people love the most. The truth is: there were people sufficiently greedy, brainwashed and/or equipped for violence who actively sold other people (usually conquered enemies from neighbouring towns) for such commodities. But most times it was not a 'trade', it was just plain old kidnapping and it was so rampant, the entirety of what we call Nigeria, Togo and Republique du Benin today was called The Slave Coast by European dealers. Entire communities were depopulated. It is important to note also, that many African chiefs refused to let slaves be taken from their people, hence the multiple British 'punitive expeditions'. The Europeans obviously had a well-oiled machine and no chief, regent or king could have masterminded that kind of wholesale trafficking and transportation of human bodies.

33: LACUNA JAMMED/ROLLED AWAY

lacuna jammed. the body takes solace in the rhythm of mythoi.

it rises in the hiss of morning air, in the electric tremor that shakes the bones of the living and

those who've died. the stone of the tomb is rolled aside. flesh remembers the light; as pulse, as river, as memory… older than memory.

it rises, and the scent of iron and myrrh climbs the spine of the world.

the sky bends low, folding around hills, and rivers weep backward into the mountains, carrying the secret names of those who slept too long…

cherubs tilt their heads, eyes of molten opal, feathers shimmering with the reflected glow of eternity;

seraphs spiral in dizzying helixes above. nephilims, deep in the shadows of hell, pause mid-stride, mouths agape…

harmmattan is over and the rainbows erupt in riotous colour. flowers spin in impossible geometry,

tulips with every hue of a dream, scented lilies, magnolias shivering under the sun's first kiss.

birds that had slept in shadow since the fall lifted into sky: the yellow-billed turaco with a crown of sun,

the trogon with its embered chest, the bushshrike
flashing like sparks across trees, and the albino
pigeon, pure as first snow…

and in the center of it all, this body takes space. the
earth exhales: a saga unfolding, a hymn in motion

life conquers even absence, even death, even despair.
lacuna rolled away.

34: CITY LIGHTS, GODDAMN

*This is a show tune, but the show hasn't been written for it, yet**

—Nina Simone

Going home? The city sits on the bones of new world
order and

binary, coding. Smart-dust probing;

exploratory, electronic, sub-atomic eyes.

All ties to the primitiveness of petroleum, gone.
Which means no

more oil wars, which means new hobbies, which
means space stations and moon bases

Earth rests a bit as there is nothing left to fight for.

Nothing left to bite for. Nothing to claim rights for.
The light for

streets are so damn bright and innately smart, guiding
turtles to certain death by flying Ubers.

Nanobots mop up all accidents with renewable
energy. Put on a glowing smile.

In room 338,000, your windows are fitted with VR
screens;

One minute you're here, and depending on where you
turn,

next you’re simulating Mars or Saturn.

Son, there are no aliens but the ones living in our
bodies.

8 billion pairs of eyes hard-wired to be second class
citizens.

Inside the city lights, since darkness is an anathema,
tired geniuses hang,

suspended from life-support machines...
Going home? No, you can’t.

Not really.

This is a show tune, but the show hasn’t been written for it, yet— a Nina Simone quote from Mississippi Goddam. Mississippi Goddam is a song responding to the murder of Medgar Evers in Mississippi and the church bombing in Alabama. The lyrics are heavy, but the music itself is upbeat and is supposed to be for a show. Here, N.S states that the show hasn't been written yet, which means that the listeners have to be the ones to write it and change the direction in which their lives are going.

35: BUSHLAND BLUES, '60.

a buffering icon spinning over the cartographer's wet dream; is it Africa, with mutants who reside in margins of the simulation? or the no-name nation that inherited its shape from some table in Berlin? perhaps it's the tribe whose tongue fits my mouth until my skin tone betrays me, or the state that didn't exist when my grandmother learned the names of landmarks? tribal marks or facial recognition technology, when new states are born, do I wake up stateless, my memories suddenly invalid, my passport a nonsense file? will flags respawn, will I feel my atoms voting without me? they tell me home is where you pay taxes, or where your ancestors are buried/enslaved*, or where your accent softens—but accents are just waveforms shaped by pressure, and graves are coordinates pretending to be permanence. physics teaches us that nothing is still: the electron field fluctuates, the vacuum boils, particles pop in and out: migrants, still we build identities as if matter itself isn't improvising. are we explaining the universe, or are we just dressing ignorance in equations, christening the costume *truth*? maybe home is quantum entanglement: something I affect even when I leave, something that collapses only when observed, something that changes depending on who is looking and why. or maybe home is the question itself, refusing to resolve, asking me back with every step forward…

Enslaved— There are families in Nigeria today comprising those who were slave traders and enablers. The Sokoto Caliphate, for example, still possessed millions of slaves as recently as the early twentieth century. In fact, there were more slaves on the local markets than could be sold, as exports of *jihad* captives had been stopped.

No name nation—"Nigeria—as we call our latest dependency—is not properly a name. It cannot be found upon a map that is ten years old. It is only an English expression which has been made to comprehend a number of native states covering about 500,000 square miles of territory in that part of the world which we call the Western Soudan. Ancient geographers called the same section of Africa sometimes Soudan, sometimes Ethiopia, sometimes Nigritia, sometimes Tekrour, sometimes and more often Genewah or Genowah—which, by the European custom of throwing the accent to the fore part of the word, has become Guinea; sometimes they called it simply Negroland. Always, and in every form, their name for it meant the Land of the Blacks. Genowah, pronounced with a hard G, is a native word signifying "black." It is so generally used to designate blacks that at the present day, among the Arabs of Egypt and the Moors of Morocco—that is, at both exits from the desert—I have myself heard it applied to the negroes of the Soudan. From the earliest periods of which we have any knowledge, Blackland has stretched, as it stretches now, from the west coast of Africa to the east, along that line of successive waterways which begins with the mouth of the Senegal, and ends only at the southern mouth of the Red Sea."

— A TROPICAL DEPENDENCY: *An Outline of the Ancient History of the Western Soudan with an Account of the Modern Settlement of Northern Nigeria* by Flora l. Shaw (Lady Lugard)

36: WHO'S GOT YOUR BACK?

Dogs is Gods backwards—

one waits beside your ruin,

one feeds on your fears.

37: THE ABOMINATION

Its one eye, a jaundiced spoiled moon, squats in the center of its face, the other side caved inward… Its body is all wrong: thin in places that should be strong, bulbous where elegance might have helped—an anthropomorphic bat stitched together by mockery and neglect. The ~~wings~~ old curtains drag when it walks, membranous and veined, and posture is permanently apologetic, hunched as though it expects to be laughed at before it speaks. Which is often. Faux pas and breathing come naturally: acyrologia, jokes that land sideways, silences held a beat too long. People snicker, and then they relax, and then they underestimate.

The showrunner dances because this abomination fancies it. Strings run from that lone, unblinking eye down into the arenas, into the lights, into the jokes that make brutality feel normal. Laughter is the most efficient anesthetic, humiliation prepares the body for obedience, spectacle is a kinder word for slaughter. And because it trips over its old curtains, because it looks like something a bored god doodled, the bat thing is so much deadlier. By the time they realize the strings are garrotes, the eye is already upon them, constantly calculating: how much pain will break you, how much spectacle will sweeten it, how long can the crowd be made to watch?

[Ugh. You don kpai?]

Patient, amused: slightly offended by their disbelief, but mostly disappointed that it took them so long to notice who was really pulling the show.

38: VILLAIN ORIGIN STORY

war as low vibration, splitting the sky. rats surged through gutters and sewers, birds ruled the air with bright, blade-winged certainty, and the bat, native of neither ground nor heaven, fought among his <cousins> with borrowed loyalty. he bit and clawed in the trenches that belonged to rats. but when the story morphed, when fate tilted toward wings and altitude, he switched allegiance and flew skyward, blood still wet on his teeth. and the clever birds saw through the performance. and the rats howled it. both armies recoiled, and for the first time their hatred aligned.

so they hunted him together.

this is why the sky spat him out. and it is why the ground would not take him back. so he embraced the <great lie> learned to love the in-between. caves. under bridge. gutters. cozy in the thundergod's latrine. neon dusk where cameras blink themselves to sleep. where the mammon system sucks meaning from labor, pleasure from compliance, terror from devotion; a perpetual, spinning ouroboros of human energy. and he leaned into the curse, crowned king of the unseen, ruling with echolocation and intel, reaching and teaching the bottom of the ladder. actively scheming for the world to go dark enough to forgive him—or dark enough to belong.

39: THE ONLY TRUE [VERIFY THIS] SACRAMENT

but the dog will sit beside you in crisis & lick the salt
from your wrists,

& the committee of thundergods internationale, or
the idea of Him

franchised across skylines,

will surprise you by harvesting that salt, distilling your
angst & fear into

glittering ambrosia, will bottle it in gold-leaf vials
labeled *Purpose* or *Test* or *Growth*,

& sell it back to you at a profit, for capitalism is their
only true sacrament

40: XOXO

tunes of a toad—
the ex was a xenopus*
x carries the trauma well, but
the monkey on y's back wears xxl

xiphoid dick:

we are the noble xe
blended in the atmosphere. xxxploited
because of what we
remember × how we remember.
every december, the chorus of the crew
causes nightmares to pirouette in view
but all the dreamers are woke now.
and all the screamers are broke now.
xenophobe on the xylophone: we x'd
the mothership after the xxth century.
circle a xerophyte* in remembrance
of sin and sinner. there is a xenial dinner
same face, same race, but with mines
in the xystus. no xenomorphs or honeybees*
allowed. defenestrate the x**ker.

the x**ker:

i have not come from
my xeric habitat to roleplay xerxes,
x—cross my heart and hope to die—x
hope that reconciliation is xenographed,

all the xylographs show
we are the result of a xenogamy of x-rated
ideas. x is plural and contested
x is plural and sun tested
x's a mural, not a xeroxed utopia
where x-men try too hard to be
xenoliths. find x in the pyramids. find x
in the tumbling cross on the deck of
the clotilda, you want revenge or restitution? think of
x as a union of opposites, x as equilibrium,
x as the spiritual jump-start for refinement, and
redefinition. the in-fighting is how they got us the
first
time; x-ray the death dealer, his first crime and
his love for the hideous.
dear xerophilous genius,
this is a xenogenesis
to defeat weaponized disunity
we must achieve a singularity
of purpose, of aim, of peaceful ruthlessness.

xo xo.

Xenopus— commonly known as the clawed frog, is a genus of highly aquatic frogs native to areas south of the Sahara. They have no vocal sacs, so they make clicks underwater. They are commonly studied as model organisms for developmental biology, cell biology, toxicology, neuroscience and for modelling human disease and birth defects, because of their powerful combination of experimental tractability and close evolutionary relationship with humans.

Xerophyte—Trees that survive with very little water. In the West African Kingdom of Dahomey, before the Kingdom's captives departed for the New World to be enslaved, they were forced to march around the 'Tree of Forgetfulness' six times so that they would remember neither their home continent nor the people they were leaving behind.

Xenomorphs or honeybees— parasitoid wasps are said to have inspired the creation of the Xenomorph alien in the movie franchise, but the South African Cape honeybee? That's another matter. These bees (Apis mellifera capensis) can create perfect copies of themselves without a Queen. With this perpetual-cloning ability, they sneak into the hives of the African lowland honeybees (Apis mellifera scutella) and churn out copy after copy of themselves. The clones are freeloaders, who just strut around refusing to do any work. They create chaos and lead to an eventual collapse of any hive they invade.

Xe— Xenon. A colorless, odorless, noble gas element found in minute quantities in the atmosphere, extracted commercially from liquefied air and used in stroboscopic, bactericidal, and laser-pumping lamps.

Xystus— (In ancient Greece) a long portico used by athletes for exercise. (In ancient Rome) a garden walk or terrace.

Xenial— Relating to, or constituting hospitality or relations between host and guest, and especially among the ancient Greeks between persons of different cities.

Clotilda—The schooner Clotilda was the last known U.S. slave ship to bring captives from West Africa (present day Republique du Benin) to the United States, arriving at Mobile Bay, in autumn 1859, with 110 kidnapped men, women, and children. After the voyage, the ship was burned and scuttled in an attempt to destroy the evidence.

Pyramids — You can find the X on the walls of a number of ancient Egyptians temples and pyramids. It is the sign of Osiris, the great sun god. The ancient pharaohs, when they were buried, had the legs crossed in the form of "X" as a sign of devotion to Osiris

---

41: HOW FAST CAN YOU GO?

Sometimes I imagine the universe as a vast clockwork orchard, where all the osan were already fallen ere the tree first hallucinated blossom, and I walk-run beneath its metallic branches wondering whether my footsteps are decisions or merely echoes traveling backward through time, whether the argument I had at noon was etched into the bones of the Big Bang like a hairline fracture waiting to widen, whether every kiss, every war, every misdialed number had to occur in the exact order they unfolded, dominoes arranged by a meticulous anarchist, and if so, what then is this sensation inside my chest that identifies as choice, this bright coin I flip in the dark believing the arc belongs to me, perhaps this is a river frozen mid-flood, and we are the fish convinced we invented swimming, or maybe this is a prism/ choreography of light, running so intricately that freedom exists in how we inhabit the steps, and the truth ≠ the path was fixed, instead = the running feels like ours. There's a ship waiting for us at the pier.

42: THIS IS NOT WAKANDA

This is not Wakanda. This is a farce.

This is tourism where alien foot prints reach

each aphorism crab-wise in verse

This is tokenism. This is futurism. This is how Prometheus' tats and

dreadlocks got a target on his arse. This is shame on the universe

This is astral engines in reverse. This is death, this is birth, this is mirth

where uncle Toms* converse.

This is looking through Tesla's field glasses in Einstein's night classes

This is àṣà àti èdè going home in a hearse. And maybe we're skirting

the realm of fantasy and wishful thinking. Maybe we're sinking

Maybe we are blinking and not really seeing the big picture.

I am using the tool of discomfiture

and orchestrated opprobrium. Can't find a loud enough Morse against the theory of Hamitic curse. Gotta make the right kind of noise as these

imbeciles voice:

[If your ancestors were so powerful, why didn't their Gods help you?]

Uncle Toms—The real life Uncle Tom was quite different from that creature in the Harriet Beecher Stowe classic. His name was Josiah Henson. In 1830, after getting fed up with his slave masters and their many broken promises, he took matters into his own hands and escaped. Stowed away to Ohio with his wife and kids on foot. Encountered Original Americans who helped him get to New York. Met some boatmen, who assisted him and his family in reaching Ontario, Canada. Afterwards, he made it part of his life's mission to free other enslaved Black folks. In addition to inspiring the novel that's been credited with ushering in the Civil War and consequently, the liberation of slaves in the U.S. His praiseworthy list of accomplishments includes rescuing One hundred and eighteen enslaved people; winning a medal at the first World's Fair; and helping to build, *Dawn*, one of the final stops on the Underground Railroad.

43: AN IDIOT'S GUIDE TO UNDERSTANDING WHY WE ARE WHERE WE ARE

RACISM:

Not tribalism, mind you. Tribalism is a small-scale colonial construct.

With no one to check their conduct, death-dealers fed on the petty coups

Of 250 ethnic groups, divided, conquered and went on their way

with merry whoops. Sixty-something years later, we still have PTSD. Racism?

'Tis the industrial, wholesale projection of anxieties, insecurities

and unadulterated hate on peoples and cultures with whom they can't relate.

And [Why?] you ask, my dear.

There's no simple answer till date. What folks don't get, they tend to fear, and try to subjugate.*

SEX:

Everything in this life is about sex, it's amusing—the drug no one admits to using.

Only sex isn't about sex, sex is about power. The Death-dealers who package and sell

de flower, be it on billboards or on the internet, are well aware of the psychology,

of human biology and the illusion of choice and control… but let the good times roll and let the prayer bells toll

for—

RELIGION:

Those calling us barbarians

Recycling 'Crusade' versus Arabians…*

'tis not to make one side look like it was dishing out lesser horrors—

just so you know, they were both bloodthirsty conquerors.

consider now how these bloodthirsty bustards split us into

segments based on dogmas not native to the continent

because people need hope.

And people need fear. And in order to cope,

paper plane escapes; violence also, is a tool for social engineering.

Allahu Akbar, Shalom and God bless your colonial leaning

pay Jesus and the government to launder your bloody linen…

But I digress, I digress—now, tell me book-walker, what's next?

MONEY:

We're Hunter-gatherers, they said. Trade by barterers, they said. Taking bread

and filling brown bellies with dread,

They taught that it made sense to collect pieces of colored paper in exchange

for cocoa or a car or a caricature. Destroyed existing

systems* just so they could create banks filled with futures

only they could manufacture...

EDUCATION:

So, you should know book-walker, Death-dealers do not teach

what they can't control. The Hafiz in the north who belts out the

entire Qur'an but cannot speak a word of English, is
still *educated.*

Just not in the way you are. Death-dealers however,
tell you

otherwise, to make you feel like a star.

Forget the toxic for a moment; hark now the visible,
undeniable beauty

in the roar of a panther crouched. No question of his
intellectual

capacity. The university

needs little literates to work the factories and mines,
but—

what are your thoughts on Nsibidi? Nok? The Yorùbá
and

their arcane technology? Olden languages and

ancient brotherhoods, our lores passed down from
sire to

son—customs outlawed for no reason

other than the fact that they are strong reminders...

The day you break free is the day you become a
marked man.

Subjugate— Author Tidiane N'Diaye estimates that 17 million East Africans were sold into slavery. 8 million Africans were brought from East Africa via the Trans-Saharan route to Morocco or Egypt. A further 9 million were deported to regions on the Red Sea or the Indian Ocean. From 1820, Omani settlers began cultivating cloves in Zanzibar to meet the growing demand on the world market. Large plantations quickly developed and slaves could be bought cheaply at the nearby slave market. At the end of August 1791, a slave revolt began in Haiti and the Dominican Republic. These two uprisings contributed to the abolition of the transatlantic slave trade. However, it was not until 1909 that Slavery was finally abolished in East Africa. We can't say the same of North Africa, though. Till today, there are still cases of enslaved black people in Libya and Mauritania.

Paper plane escapes—If the crusades have any lesson to teach us it is this: mixing myths (or historical fantasies) with politics leads only to calamity.

An existing system—Africans had developed currency before the death dealers came. The Okpogho people of Enugu State for instance, were West Africa's first mint. They manufactured a metal currency that only they issued, unlike the manilla that was largely made in Europe.

44: BEFORE/AFTER GOD LEARNT TO BREATHE FIRE

I'll sing to you, a song from the old days.

Here, Oyo is young, and what the king says

is law: his wrath lays its paw on strong

and weak, double-bladed, calibrated

to both punish and awe, but he hungers

for more, for power not measurable

in mere fear or obedience, and the score

is for a thrill that requires the skill

of old Èṣù, the master of crossroads

Èṣù most clever, Èṣù whose force loads

the mundane and crafts it into weapons

who lives in the interstitial sections

of red and black, and order and chaos,

the worrier god peers down upon us:

and this king, Ṣàngó, sends his messengers

they search high and low, cross lands and rivers,

ignoring the ordinary healers

and juju men hard-boiled in the blue mud

seeking the who? [god] who alone knows the

medicine. And they find his venison

hung to cure, in this huge courtyard and the

person that approaches diminutive

intuitive, chief dialectitian

and he tells them [I know why you have come

and from whence, and I sure can prepare your

medicine, but you must send the king's wife

to come collect in a fortnight] and they

nodding their thanks, depart quick from thence, for

Eṣù short and mighty's mood could change course

the worrier god peers down upon us:

and the Oba sends his most athletic,
Oya. Who'd make the trip look pathetic
and the medicine would be wrapped in a
packet so seemingly innocuous it
could be mistaken for dust, and Oya
the impatient and curious, would feel
fire spring in her throat when brushing tongue
against it, but she delivers it like that
and the king, sensing an imperfection
in procedure, consumes some himself from
high above his city, exhaling flames
that leap and coil like serpents, igniting
straw roofs and granaries, scattering sheep
into death while Oya hides beneath them,
Oyo becomes ash… but time does not pause
the worrier god peers down upon us:

And, long after Oyo, Digi City
emerged. A ditty of glass and metal
forests full of petal after petal
of petabytes of data. Holograms
and biograms that hummed soft like living
electricity, and Ṣàngó switched their
axe for algorithms, and their hot wrath
came as viral storms and trending crises,
and old Èṣù migrated too, waiting
salivating, as the cycles go from pisces
to leo, or whatever, per the sky lark—
home is the question mark hovering above
ruin and reconstruction, safety is
supposition, loyalty is measured
in attention spans/click-throughs, and chaos…
the worrier god peers down upon us.

45: BRIDGING DISTANCE

Melanin is worth more than gold on the black
market.* Black

is beautiful, even when it is swallowing up amalgams

for mis-identification. These are the crimes of mass
education.

Anarchist? No. I'm not about to evangelize or quote
long-dead

Pharaohs & their pyramids at you. I made my peace
with the

fact that there was a war my father lost. But the future
is only

the past re-entered through another gate & you can't
drive if

you're only ever looking in the rear-view mirror.

Mindless fun is how they get us… but go on, Book-
walker.

Wormholes or Kánàkò? To hitch a ride home, we grit
our

teeth & squeeze our sphincters.

Once,

I was invited to an owambe. Gele of many colours towering, screaming [oh, I'm here] ample hips, big as kingdoms, swaying; the Fuji tribute band on some vibes and wisdom playing, the speakers carving grooves into the asphalt, the asphalt carrying the weight of the dancers, the dancers struggling with the oil stained hands of children clutching zobo bottles. & what's a party without the fighting for food? The MC was yabbing everyone, her improv was good. Amala & abula wafted through the air, & there was the smoky scent of party jollof. All of the women's laughter ricocheted off the walls; the elders in buba and overalls, sipped palm wine & smiled their approval per secret-holders. *Eeju o*, you greet & go to get some peppered snail, or ponmo, or steaming bowl of egunfe. Where do you think you are? You never say [no] to your in-law's cooking! The music will shift to apala & you'll sway in it, your own chest rising, inhaling the scent of spices & sun, understanding that the world can be burned down, rebuilt, & still rise like these hips, these gele towers, these songs of joy and celebration…

Man,

This sh—t is crazy. We are now in an age where we can be using hypersonic

spaceliners to bridge great distances, yet we're unable to bridge our differences.

Melanin, as at the time of writing this, is actually worth more than gold on the black market. * Melanin goes for $428.00 a gram. Gold is $44.90 per gram.

46: BLACK PROTOCOL

[But how does one triumph, Book-walker?]

By understanding one's environment and one's self;

constant but shifting coordinates—be kind to all.
Including your subordinates

There is no monolithic experience, but there'll always
be

Black sheep. Black tragedy. Black bleep in the bights
of

Biafra and Benin. Black Identity Extremist—Black
labels,

broad labels, Black Abels. Kinky hair and Black eyed
sins

Twisted into joyless mannequins. Must reject this
eternal ennui. Must reject this

prison of language, this Graveyard bureau de Change
where there's only squalor for

[*People of* color,]* kú ise o—genius, as you have seen
people

who have no color

[And how do we reconfigure this marker, Ògún?]

[We start by refusing to shut up.]

People of Color—a term used by death dealers to erase identity. It's supposedly progressive and PC but what it really does is depict historically excluded people and people of non-white descent as a monolith. Benevolent racism at its peak.

Kú iṣẹ o— Yoruba phrase said in a sarcastic way to mean "well done o"

47: 1885*

The mortar (odò) will bear witness

that I see room in which to (dò) *settle*, the tètè leaf

will bear witness that I see space in which to (te) *spread*,

the gbégbé* leaf will bear witness that I see home in which to

(gbé)* live. Omi* is sacrificed so that my offspring can mi*—

Who then are these who rise up to pull down?

The shell of a groundnut looks exactly like the coffin

of the smallest rat—

<!--[if 8] = [wholeness] [3 is one half of a sequence/

</dodging> </><![charm]--><!--[has mandated you]

<not to> <dodge> <my><Command>[33.8][33.8]

<deathdealers><deathdealers><ofo><c:charmsettings>

<gods> <since> <1885> <ashatteringofcentralnetwork>

</w:View> <w:zoom>0</w:Zoom> </w:view>

<w:trackmoves></w:trackmoves></ [track] Àpadà

</the changing leaf]><--[has mandated you]><not to>

<change> <what>/I say!]>{lore}<tortoise ><Ṣìgìdì>

<dancingpalmtree><w:trackformat></w:trackformat>

<w:breakwarpedtables><w:warpedlogic><teardownstatues>

<w:validateagainstschemers></w:validateagainstschemers>

<thethingsthatfellapart></w:金繕い [commandeer]<their>

<tech<w:ignoremixedcontent>/w:IgnoreFalseContent>

<Akese always has the>[final]<say in the midst of cotton>

="true" name="heading 8"> <w:deception locked="false"

priority locked="false" priority="8" qformat="true"

name="heading 8"> <w: 8"><Hivemind interconnectivity>

<w:deception = trust ="false" priority="33.8" name = "Brit">

<w:deception =trust="false" priority="33.8" name="Dutch">

<w:deception [trust]="false" priority="33.8" name="Potoki*">

<w:deception [trust]="false" priority="33.8" name="Faransé">

<w:deception = trust="false" priority="33.8" name="Germ.">

<w:deception [trust] ="false" priority="33.8" name = "Belg.">

<w:deception = trust ="false" priority="33.8" name="S.pain">

Whatever command òkété* issues to the ground,

is what the ground obeys. Àṣẹ.

1885 is the year of the infamous Berlin conference, where western super powers (including Turkey) divided Africa on a map and claimed territories for themselves.

Gbegbe— *Icacina trichantha*, a drought-resistant medicinal plant.

Omi—the Yorùbá word for 'water'.

Mi—the Yorùbá word for 'breathe'.

Potoki—slang name for the Portuguese. In the Bight of Benin, the Portuguese were responsible for more than half the total figure of 'exported' slaves, during the second half of the 1670s. Then followed the French (from 1704). Then the English, of course. Then the Spanish (but only from 1800), and the Dutch (taking as much as they could in the 17th century only to disappear completely shortly after). Then finally, far behind, came Denmark-Norway and Brandenburg-Prussia.

Dancing palm tree—this is a reference to an old folktale about Ìjàpá the tortoise who enchants a palm tree and makes it dance violently in the middle of the marketplace. Traders, frightened by the sight, flee leaving their wares; and as soon as the place is quiet, Ijapa loots their stalls. He does this again and again, until the villagers decide they have had enough. A wise woman advices them to mould a Ṣìgìdì, and place it in the center of the market. They do this, but flee as usual the next time Ijapa does his dancing palm tree trick. The tortoise mistakes the lone figure for a trader refusing to run. Fuelled by hubris, he confronts the Ṣìgìdì but finds himself glued to the thing. He is unable to extricate himself until the villagers return to the market, to find that he is the culprit.

金繕い— Kintsukuroi, the Japanese art of mending broken pottery with gold.

òkété—a species of bush rat with white-tipped tail. It has such uncanny human-like attributes; some Yorùbá believe it is the re-incarnation of the warrior ancestor Oníkòyí.

eye of the worrier god *peering down upon us.*

48: AND YET IT REMAINS BLUE

the water carries suicides/ juju-tied lovers, soft bodies folding into its vernacular,/ swallows evidence with a patient mouth/and far below where photosynthesis' all but given up,/ undiscovered phyla blink in bioluminescent morse code…

epics about the rise and fall of empires that never once thanked them for oxygen; and is it still progress when you pour your waste into her veins, just so you can shoot rockets at the sky and puncture heaven for sport?

we should be more mindful. dinosaurs pressed into the seabed have bones fluent in fallout, they know that extinction is really a re-rehearsal, where ash falls eventually on everything that believes itself untouchable; the water has watched continents rearrange their furniture, has learned the flavor of ambition, and still it moves with deceptive gentleness, touching your ankles as like a courteous host, reflecting your face as if it does not know what you have done, but do not mistake the mirror for mercy, for the water is alive with a patience older than language, and it is waiting for you to remember that you are mostly made of it.

i will offer to Yemoja, i will offer gently, without littering devotion across the beach. orange slices, melon cubes, berries, grapes, pineapple, i will tell her these are gifts swollen with their own small oceans, i will let a few pieces drift into her palm, and i will carry the rest away,

i will craft new oriki/ for those whose names became currents in the middle passage,/ and i will thank the queen of the sea/ for holding hulls together with invisible hands,/ for carrying both the living and the lost,/ for being home even when home was unthinkable…

and i will thank Olókun, for the stability that arrived in my life, for shelter that rose from nowhere, for the talent that held me steady when i was seventeen and unmoored, for the way foundations form in silence far below spectacle, for Olókun does not hunger for the sweetness arranged on porcelain, they hunger for depth, for weight, for the honest smell of things returning to themselves; fish decaying, dissolving to salt

breathing elegance of the sea, which remembers everything and yet remains blue.

49: JUMPING SHIP

The air shivers like a live wire above the pier,

lagoon roiling beneath, and then it comes into view, impossibly high,

the bat, the puppeteer's puppeteer, tier upon tier,

Thor's eyes are fissures in ice

beard cascading snow and god-lice

and behind them the Committee of Trouble Internationale: Baal, Jupiter, Zeus, Perun, Leigong, Donar, Teshub, Taranis—

laughing a latticework of cannon fire

the pier's wood groaning, why do they move as though 1884 never ended?

and I feel the weight of it pressing into my chest,

my rage rising like magma, centrifugal, screaming through my blood:

I know I am not free, and it makes me so angry.

and my lover's beside me, hair slick with sweat and wrath,

and the dog is beside us alert, muscles tight, teeth bared, as a plus

and the water's slapping wood in a slow, obscene applause,

why i dunno

this is my family: *they* come as a committee, why should we face them solo?

it's a lightbulb moment that becomes megawatts and megawatts of focused beams

and the bat screams,

and his terrified decibels swell air and water and memory,

then bursts—flesh and myth and machinery,

and splatters—ichor, contracts, old bones, and nullified curses

and the thundergods tuck in their phalluses

they perform their final attempts at being proud

into the lagoon with a sound too small for a life so loud,

and we run, leap, jump—a money shot etched into the future,

and the ship waiting for us, reveals itself

and the ship waiting for us, reveals itself.

THE BEGINNING.

HANNU AFERE is an author and animator and whose work explores the speculative using the vehicles of Yorùbá spirituality and future science. His work has appeared in several publications in Nigeria, Brazil, China, Germany, Canada and the US.

He co-authored the critically acclaimed graphic novel *Trinity: Red October* in 2018, and wrote the screenplay to *The Adventures of Captain Blud,* an animated series with the Nobel Laureate Professor Wole Soyinka in 2021.

Presently, he is the Editor-in-chief of *the Anthology of West African Literature* (8th House Publishing, Montréal). *Go Home* is his first full length book of poems.

50: ONE LAST SONG TO TAKE YOU HOME

Dunbar Creek.

You sit with your family*, communicating with your eyes only. Captain Patterson* makes you irate, him and his little band of glorified pirates. He barks orders and sparks murder in the scowl of your mother.

Outside, the sea would rise and fall, like the timbre of dirges on all. *Lightning and foamy brine;* there's a chill crawling down your spine—

Two things that could occur in this situation, as you're nearing destination; for the ship will not hold. To follow your mother bold, go to 6. To follow the captain, head to 3.

1. You are a Water-Treader*. Under the rock, led by the Mammy Wota girl, you find yourself where two portals swirl; one pulsates like the beating heart of a bird, the other one is a gate of fire. To enter the pulsating portal, go to 11. To enter the fire, go to 2.

2. It should be self-immolation, but you do not burn. And you do not turn. You count 74* souls, the soles of their feet caressing water like native language. It is

a tragic voyage, and lord alone knows why it is happening. You want to ask him? Why he let you go through hell, through this darkest hour? Why he let you suffer if he could give you such special power? You want to go ask him? Proceed to 10.

3. You follow Captain Patterson in his dirty blue coat into this creaky old boat. He smells of putrefaction and gin. You have no illusions what these mean. As he rows for shore, you say [No one can blame me, for a living dog is better than a dead lion.] To disembark meekly into Babylon, go to 4. To change your mind and make for shore on your own, go to 7.

4. As soon as you set foot on dry land, you see the law-twisting brigand and their redneck uncles with worse than manacles—jars of your future fetuses germinate out of their head. They're waiting, salivating. You are alive, and yet you are dead.

5. Welcome to the place of No Beginning. There is no conceivable way to get here. How you take do am? The matrix is impressed.

6. Your mother is humming a familiar tune, *orimiri omambala bu anyi bia/ orimiri omambala ka anyi ga ejina**. The others start to sing. You see Fat Roswell King

who is screaming for all to scram, who is shrieking to leave the ship while you still can. To heed his advice, go to 3. To stay put, plant a foot in 14.

7. You dive into the murky waters with a great big splash. It's brash, but you stroke your best. East or West? To swim east, go to 8. To head swim west, go to 9.

8. You have some experience swimming. You were never champion back home, but under your dome there is the mentality of winning. Yonder, behind the jutting rock, is a long-haired girl of Mammy Wota* stock. She beckons with eye-lid flutter and you discover you can walk on water. To chase after her, go to 1. To heave yourself out of the marsh, go to 12.

9. You can't even see where you're going. Water finds its way into your nostrils and lungs. You still hear the processional songs, but there's no one to right or write these wrongs. Pebble in Atlantic bucket, you kick and hit the water bed. Down, down, down and down—oh wow, now you are proper dead.

10. Whirlpool, maelstrom—the Mammy Wota girl points to a gigantic mother of pearl. You enter and see the lord sitting calmly in the Vortices. Cortices of

the seventy-four plead tearfully that you tread carefully, dear. But you are boiling with a rage you didn't even know was there. This figure has only one leg and his head has a balding patch. Angrily, you challenge the lord to a wrestling match, (in 13). Or you ask your question genuflecting, reflecting some home training in 15.

11. You are ejected towards the purple sky as a buzzard*. Your wings buzz hard on their own accord, lifting you up and away beyond the ghostly fjord. You escape capture, but are *still* a grotesque vulture. They *will* sing songs about you many years after, and we *still* hear the resounding echoes of your maniacal laughter.

12. [Not today, Satan] you murmur. You have heard it told before, how the Mammy Wota lure men to death's watery door. Exhausted to the core, you find that that Roswell boor is patiently waiting for you by the shore. He calls you a racist slur, whacks you in the skull and the rest is a blur. When you awake, your entire body's so frigging sore. He gets 10 credits for your head. You certainly wish you were dead.

13. The lord accepts your challenge. If you win, you can bend Time and Space to circumvent this mess. If you lose, you'll be reduced to disgusting fish food or something even less. He advances. You shoot for the leg on which he balances. Throw him over your hip

and his back touches the ground. Then you bring your fists up and start to pound. Congratulations. A Jacob's come to town. Reverse this timeline and re-berth. Reverse this timeline and… Re: Birth.

14. You run your finger along a shelf. The wood starts to cave in on itself. The sheer sonic energy of the chant causes The Morovia* to implode. Three white overseers scream as their bodies disintegrate and their skulls pop like bad fruits squashed. You look towards your mother, but she is gone. Everyone's gone. You smile contentedly, and walk with folded arms into sea. *"The Water Spirit brought us; the Water Spirit will take us home"*.

15. The lord sighs in exasperation, at your stupidity. Your humility is born of mere desperation. About your question, there is no *simple* answer… but whachoo gon' do abourrit? You start to stammer and fumble, but he doesn't let you land. He spits you out onto the far side of the cursed island where the cannibalistic capitalists wait to harvest your genitals, brain and hand.

Family–In May 1803, a group of 75 enslaved Igbo people were bought by agents of John Couper and Thomas Spalding for forced labor on their plantations in St. Simons Island for $100 each.

The following sequence of events is unclear, as there are several versions of the revolt's development, some of which are considered mythological. Apparently, the Africans went ashore and subsequently, under the direction of their leader, walked in unison into the creek singing in the Igbo language "The Water Spirit brought us, the Water Spirit will take us home". They thereby accepted the protection of Chukwu and death over the alternative of slavery.

Chukwu—the Almighty, Supreme Being in Igbo tradition.

Roswell King—the person who recovered the bodies of the drowned.

Mammy Wota—female water spirits, having the upper body of an attractive woman and generally with fish tails. Sometimes though, the bottom half is that of a snake.

Buzzard—This was recorded from various oral sources in the 1930s by members of the Federal Writers Project: Wallace Quarterman, an African American born in 1844, who was interviewed in 1930, when asked if he had heard about the Igbo landing is quoted as saying, *"Ain't you heard about them? Well, at that time Mr. Blue he was the overseer and ... Mr. Blue he go down one morning with a long whip for to whip them good. ... Anyway, he whipped them good and they got together and stuck that hoe in the field and then ... rose up in the sky and turned themselves into buzzards and flew right back to Africa. ... Everybody knows about them."*

The Morovia— or The Schooner York according to some sources. The vessel carrying the crime.

Orimiri Omambala—The water spirit Omambala which was mispronounced by colonialists as Anambra. A quick google search however shows another account of this story. Attributing it to the spirit of the Imo River which runs between present day Imo State and Abia. It runs into the Atlantic between a section of Rivers State and Akwa Ibom State in Nigeria. She is usually feminine and was associated with the Ibinukpabi oracle or "Long Juju" of Arochukwu, the most powerful oracle in southeastern

Nigeria during the Atlantic Slave Trade, and she is considered as its female counterpart.

A SHORT LIST OF THE PEOPLE I'D LIKE TO THANK

First of all, I'd like to thank Vivian Okwuagwu, you lit a spark in me during a period of bleakness, and our conversations about legacy and spirituality, I'll never forget. You're a god-send.

Special thanks to Ala Africa and Uzoma Kelvin Alaneme for being the Q to my James Bond. Your meticulousness ensured that this dream was put directly into people's hands.

I'd like to thank Bryan Thao Worra for introducing me to a whole new world in America. I'm appreciative of *Sahtu press* for giving me the opportunity with *XOXO* that got me a Rhysling nomination.

I am grateful to Tade Ipadeola for encouraging me to develop and show off my Yorùbá. I am also grateful to Chuma Nwokolo for offering early constructive criticism.

Thank you, Richard Ali, and thank you Iquo DianaAbasi, for being such amazing pre-pub readers.

I cannot thank Dhee Sylvester enough for the cover design of *Go Home.* I owe you a bottle of champagne.

On Facebook where my early career kicked off, I have had upwards of 10,000 readers. You all spring fresh surprises on me every day. Thank you, Nkiru Njoku, for your words of encouragement, you have a special place in my heart. Temi Dayo, thank you for the love, and for teaching me 'orchestrated opprobrium'. Hymar 'Ọmò Igbo' Idibie, I thank whatever possessed you to pick up the pen that first time. Ebuka Igbokwe, The body of Hannu salutes you. Deep soul thanks to Sapphire McLaniyi.

This list would be incomplete without the acknowledgement of my better half, Ebimo, who reads with me, gets reads for me and totally reads me. For the days when I had all but given up, thank you for giving me a reason to soldier on. I love you.

My deepest thanks to all those not mentioned here, who have been instrumental to the creation of this book, one way or the other. May the universe be kind to you all always.

www.ingramcontent.com/pod-product-compliance
Lightning Source LLC
LaVergne TN
LVHW090529110826
845146LV00003B/1038

* 9 7 9 8 9 9 2 7 4 4 8 2 8 *